Inside the US Navy

Jennifer Boothroyd

Lerner Publications • Minneapolis

For United States Navy families

Lerner Publications Company
A division of Lerner Publishing Group, Inc.
241 First Avenue North
Minneapolis, MN 55401 USA

For reading levels and more information, look up this title at www.lernerbooks.com.

Library of Congress Cataloging-in-Publication Data

Names: Boothroyd, Jennifer, 1972- author.
Title: Inside the US Navy / Jennifer Boothroyd.
Description: Minneapolis : Lerner Publications, [2017] | Series: Lightning bolt books. US Armed
    Forces | Includes bibliographical references and index. | Audience: Grades K-3.
Identifiers: LCCN 2016038211 (print) | LCCN 2016038344 (ebook) | ISBN 9781512433944
    (library binding : alk. paper) | ISBN 9781512450699 (eb pdf)
Subjects: LCSH: United States. Navy—Juvenile literature.
Classification: LCC VA58.4 .B685 2017 (print) | LCC VA58.4 (ebook) | DDC 359.00973—dc23

LC record available at https://lccn.loc.gov/2016038211

Manufactured in the United States of America
1-42030-23900-10/20/2016

Table of Contents

What is the US Navy?

The US Navy protects the United States by sea. It is in charge of keeping US ships safe. The navy is one branch of the US military.

The navy is ready for combat under the water too. Navy submarines sail all around the world.

Navy ships are at sea for three to nine months.

Most people in the navy spend time on ships. A sailor's day is divided into shifts. Sailors have time to work, relax, eat, and sleep.

Navy Training

Recruits must be trained to become sailors in the US Navy. Most recruits go to boot camp at a navy training center in Illinois.

Recruits are navy sailors in training.

For about eight weeks at boot camp, recruits learn to follow commands. They work as a team. They gain skills needed to sail ships.

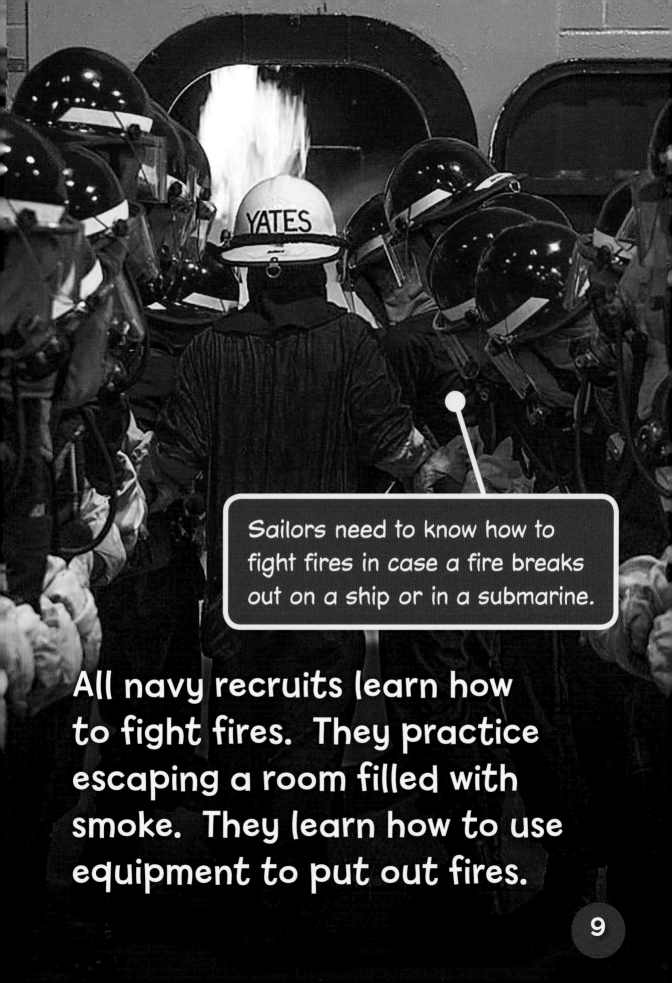

Sailors need to know how to fight fires in case a fire breaks out on a ship or in a submarine.

All navy recruits learn how to fight fires. They practice escaping a room filled with smoke. They learn how to use equipment to put out fires.

A test called battle stations is the final exam for recruit training. The test happens on a full-size model of a navy ship called the USS *Trayer*.

This officer oversees recruits on the USS *Trayer* with the help of computers.

Recruits go through practice tests that are similar to this one.

The test gives recruits a chance to practice dealing with real-life combat situations. Rooms in the USS *Trayer* can catch fire or even flood with water.

Navy Equipment

Sailors need different gear to do their jobs safely. Sailors working near loud engines wear earmuffs. And their colorful clothing allows people to see them easily and avoid accidents.

The color of the sailors' clothing differs depending on their job.

Divers wear harnesses so helicopters can lift them out of the water.

The navy has many different kinds of ships. Some submarines can stay underwater for months. Tugboats are some of the smallest ships in the navy.

A tugboat (*left*) guides the cruiser USS *Cowpens* (*right*) into a navy base after the cruiser has come back from sea.

Aircraft carriers are like floating towns.

Aircraft carriers are some of the navy's largest ships. They carry sailors, vehicles, and other equipment all around the world.

Jets take off and land from the deck on ships and aircraft carriers.

The navy uses aircraft as well as ships. Helicopters and jets are part of many missions.

The Navy of the Future

The navy is working on new ways to keep the country and its sailors safe. Robots can work in rooms filled with deadly gas and smoke. They might be used as firefighters on ships.

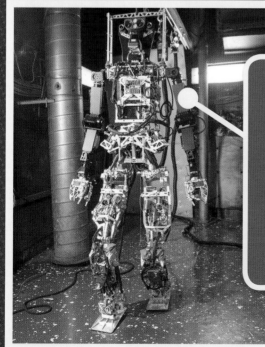

The Shipboard Autonomous Firefighting Robot (SAFFiR) may be used to help sailors fix damage or inspect navy ships.

Drones are another part of the navy's future. Drones are remote-controlled aircraft. They are safer than jets because drones don't need pilots.

Some types of drones are being used as replacements for missiles.

The sailors of the US Navy work together to protect people in the United States and around the world.

Navy Diver Gear Diagram

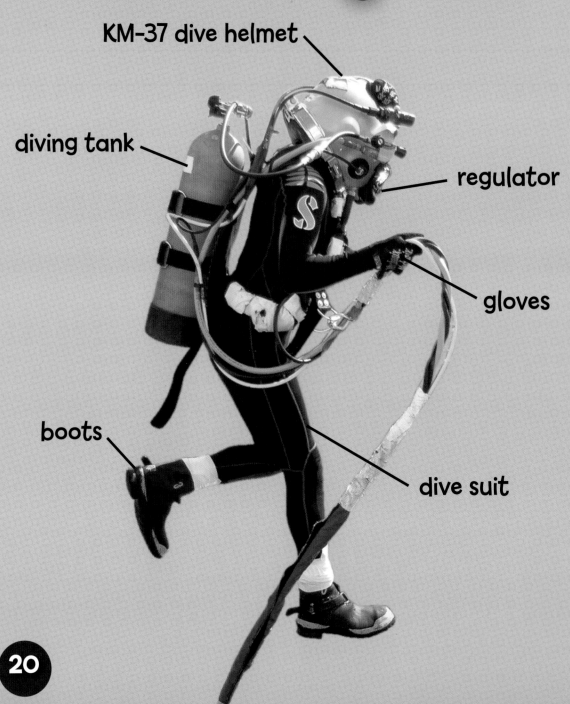

KM-37 dive helmet

diving tank

regulator

gloves

boots

dive suit

US Navy History

- The Continental navy fought during the American Revolution (1775-1783). The permanent US Navy was created in 1794.

- During the US Civil War (1861-1865), the North and South both had an ironclad ship. During a battle in 1862, neither ship could damage the other. Eventually, they stopped fighting and just left the area.

- Women first joined the navy in World War I (1914-1918), but they couldn't serve as sailors. They worked in jobs that supported sailors. Today, women can serve in all navy jobs.

Glossary

boot camp: the eight-week training after joining the US Navy

combat: fighting in a war

drone: a remote-controlled aircraft

harness: a set of straps that are used to attach a person to something, such as a rope to lift the person

recruit: a person training to be a sailor

sailor: a person who works on a boat or ship as part of the crew

tugboat: a small, powerful boat that is used to push or pull a larger ship

Further Reading

America's Navy: Life on a Sub
http://www.navy.com/navy-life/life-on-a-sub
.html#why-live-on-a-sub

America's Navy: US Navy Ships
http://www.navy.mil/navydata/our_ships.asp

Harasymiw, Mark A. *Heroes of the US Navy*. New York: Gareth Stevens, 2013.

Miller, Nancy. *My Mom Is in the Navy*. New York: PowerKids, 2016.

Newman, Patricia. *Navy SEALs: Elite Operations*. Minneapolis: Lerner Publications, 2014.

Pelleschi, Andrea. *Mathematician and Computer Scientist Grace Hopper*. Minneapolis: Lerner Publications, 2017.

Index

Photo Acknowledgments

The images in this book are used with the permission of: US Navy photo by Mass Communication Specialist 3rd Class Sean Furey/Released, pp. 2, 20; US Navy photo by Mass Communication Specialist 3rd Class Mutis A. Capizz, pp. 4, 23; US Navy photo by Mass Communication Specialist 3rd Class Sean M. Castellano, p. 5; US Navy photo by Mass Communication Specialist 1st Class James R. Evans, p. 6; US Navy photo by Mass Communication Specialist 1st Class Richard Perez, p. 7; US Navy photo by Lt. Liza Swart, p. 8; US Navy photo by Mass Communication Specialist 1st Class Chris Laurent, p. 9; US Navy photo by Brian Walsh, p. 10; US Navy photo by Mass Communication Specialist 3rd Class Adelola O. Tinubu, p. 11; US Navy photo by Mass Communication Specialist 2nd Class Nicholas Frank Cottone, p. 12; © US Navy Photo/Alamy, p. 13; US Navy photo by Mass Communication Specialist 3rd Class Will Gaskill, p. 14; US Navy photo by Mass Communication Specialist 3rd Class Nathan Burke, p. 15; US Navy photo by Mass Communication Specialist 3rd Class Casey J. Hopkins, p. 16; US Navy photo by John F. Williams, p. 17; US Navy photo by Mass Communication Specialist 3rd Class Amanda S. Kitchne, p. 18; US Navy photo by Mass Communication Specialist 3rd Class Ryan D. McLearnon, p. 19.

Front cover: Photo courtesy of General Dynamics Bath Iron Works.

Main body text set in Billy Infant regular 28/36. Typeface provided by SparkType.